Rosacea Diet

A Beginner's Guide to Managing Rosacea Through Diet, With Sample Recipes and a 5-Step Plan

mf

copyright © 2024 Mary Golanna

All rights reserved No part of this book may be reproduced, or stored in a retrieval system, or transmitted in any form or by any means, electronic, mechanical, photocopying, recording, or otherwise, without express written permission of the publisher.

Disclaimer

By reading this disclaimer, you are accepting the terms of the disclaimer in full. If you disagree with this disclaimer, please do not read the guide.

All of the content within this guide is provided for informational and educational purposes only, and should not be accepted as independent medical or other professional advice. The author is not a doctor, physician, nurse, mental health provider, or registered nutritionist/dietician. Therefore, using and reading this guide does not establish any form of a physician-patient relationship.

Always consult with a physician or another qualified health provider with any issues or questions you might have regarding any sort of medical condition. Do not ever disregard any qualified professional medical advice or delay seeking that advice because of anything you have read in this guide. The information in this guide is not intended to be any sort of medical advice and should not be used in lieu of any medical advice by a licensed and qualified medical professional.

The information in this guide has been compiled from a variety of known sources. However, the author cannot attest to or guarantee the accuracy of each source and thus should not be held liable for any errors or omissions.

You acknowledge that the publisher of this guide will not be held liable for any loss or damage of any kind incurred as a result of this guide or the reliance on any information provided within this guide. You acknowledge and agree that you assume all risk and responsibility for any action you undertake in response to the information in this guide.

Using this guide does not guarantee any particular result (e.g., weight loss or a cure). By reading this guide, you acknowledge that there are no guarantees to any specific outcome or results you can expect.

All product names, diet plans, or names used in this guide are for identification purposes only and are the property of their respective owners. The use of these names does not imply endorsement. All other trademarks cited herein are the property of their respective owners.

Where applicable, this guide is not intended to be a substitute for the original work of this diet plan and is, at most, a supplement to the original work for this diet plan and never a direct substitute. This guide is a personal expression of the facts of that diet plan.

Where applicable, persons shown in the cover images are stock photography models and the publisher has obtained the rights to use the images through license agreements with third-party stock image companies.

Table of Contents

Introduction   7
What Is Rosacea?   10
   Types of Rosacea   10
   Symptoms of Rosacea   13
   Causes of Rosacea   14
   Medical Treatments for Rosacea   16
   How to Diagnose Rosacea?   19
   Natural Remedies for Treating Rosacea   20
Managing Rosacea Through Diet   23
   Principles of The Rosacea Diet   23
   Benefits of the Rosacea Diet   25
   Potential Drawbacks of the Rosacea Diet   27
Managing Rosacea Through Lifestyle Changes   29
   Stress Management   29
   Skincare Routines   30
   Avoiding Environmental Triggers   31
   Importance of Regular Exercise   32
5-Step Plan to Get Started for Managing Rosacea Through Diet and Lifestyle Adjustments   33
   Step 1: Identify and Avoid Trigger Foods   33
   Step 2: Incorporate Anti-Inflammatory Foods   40
   Step 3: Stay Hydrated   44
   Step 4: Adopt a Gentle Skincare Routine   48
   Step 5: Manage Stress   53
   Foods to Eat   56
   Foods to Avoid   59
7-Day Sample Meal Plan   62
Sample Recipes   67
   Oatmeal with Blueberries and Chia Seeds   68

Quinoa Salad	69
Grilled Salmon with Roasted Vegetables	70
Baked Chicken Breast with Steamed Broccoli	71
Turkey and Avocado Wrap	72
Grilled Shrimp with Quinoa	73
Lentil Soup with a Side of Mixed Green Salad	75
Baked Cod with Sweet Potato Mash and Sautéed Kale	77
Turkey Meatballs with Zucchini Noodles	79
Grilled Chicken Caesar Salad with a Light Vinaigrette	81
Sweet Potato and Black Bean Tacos	83
Conclusion	**86**
FAQs	**89**
References and Helpful Links	**92**

Introduction

Millions of people around the world face the daily challenges of Rosacea, a chronic skin condition that manifests as persistent redness, visible blood vessels, and acne-like bumps primarily on the face. This condition not only affects the skin but also has a profound impact on emotional well-being, often leading to decreased self-esteem and confidence. Understanding that Rosacea is more than just a skin issue is the first step towards managing it effectively. For many, the journey to better skin health begins with a closer look at their diet.

Rosacea's exact cause remains elusive, but it's widely acknowledged that a combination of genetic, environmental, and lifestyle factors contributes to its development. Among these, diet plays a crucial role. Certain foods can exacerbate symptoms, while others can help reduce inflammation and promote healthier skin. This Rosacea Diet Guide aims to shed light on how dietary changes can make a significant difference in managing this condition.

Food is more than just fuel for the body; it can either be a friend or a foe for those with Rosacea. By understanding which foods to embrace and which to avoid, individuals can take proactive steps toward reducing flare-ups and maintaining clearer skin. This guide will provide insights into the best foods for Rosacea, explain why certain foods trigger symptoms, and offer practical tips for incorporating beneficial foods into daily meals.

A day where the redness and discomfort of Rosacea are no longer a constant concern can be within reach. By making informed dietary choices, this vision can become a reality. The Rosacea Diet Guide is designed to empower individuals with the knowledge and tools needed to make these choices confidently. Whether it's selecting anti-inflammatory foods, understanding the impact of hydration, or learning about the role of gut health, this guide covers all the essential aspects of a diet that supports skin health.

Consider the relief of enjoying meals without the fear of triggering a flare-up. By following the recommendations in this guide, individuals can experience fewer symptoms and a greater sense of control over their condition. This isn't about a temporary fix; it's about adopting sustainable dietary habits that lead to long-term improvements in skin health and overall well-being.

In this guide, we will talk about the following;

- What is Rosacea?
- Managing Rosacea Through Diet and Lifestyle Changes
- 5-Step Plan to Get Started for Managing Rosacea Through Diet and Lifestyle Adjustments
- Foods To Eat and To Avoid
- 7-Day Sample Meal Plan for Managing Rosacea
- Sample Recipes

By the end of this guide, readers will have a comprehensive understanding of how diet influences Rosacea and will be equipped with practical strategies to implement these changes. Embrace the opportunity to take control of your skin health through informed dietary choices. Start the journey towards clearer skin and improved well-being today.

What Is Rosacea?

Rosacea is a chronic skin condition that primarily affects the face, leading to visible redness and often impacting an individual's confidence and emotional well-being. While it varies in severity, Rosacea can significantly influence daily life, making social interactions and self-esteem challenging for many. Understanding Rosacea and recognizing its impacts are crucial steps toward managing the condition and improving quality of life. By raising awareness and fostering a supportive community, those affected can find effective ways to navigate and alleviate the challenges Rosacea presents.

Types of Rosacea

Rosacea is a complex skin condition that can manifest in several different forms. Each type has its own set of characteristics and symptoms, which can help in diagnosing and treating the condition effectively. Here are the primary types of rosacea:

1. **Erythematotelangiectatic Rosacea (ETR)**

   This type of rosacea is characterized by persistent facial redness and visible blood vessels. The redness often appears on the central part of the face, including the cheeks, nose, chin, and forehead. Individuals with ETR may experience frequent flushing and a burning or stinging sensation. The skin may also become dry and scaly. ETR is often the mildest form of rosacea but can progress if not managed properly.

2. **Papulopustular Rosacea**

   Papulopustular rosacea is often mistaken for acne due to the presence of red, swollen bumps (papules) and pus-filled pimples (pustules). These breakouts typically occur on the central face and are accompanied by persistent redness. Unlike acne, papulopustular rosacea does not have blackheads. This type can be particularly distressing as it affects the skin's appearance and can be painful. It is more common in middle-aged women.

3. **Phymatous Rosacea**

   Phymatous rosacea is characterized by thickened skin and a bumpy texture. The most notable feature is rhinophyma, a condition where the skin on the nose becomes thickened and enlarged, leading to a bulbous appearance. This type is more common in men and can also affect the forehead, chin, cheeks, and ears. The skin may appear oily and pores can become more prominent. Phymatous rosacea tends to develop slowly over time and may require surgical intervention for treatment.

4. Ocular Rosacea

Ocular rosacea affects the eyes and eyelids. Symptoms include redness, dryness, irritation, and a gritty sensation in the eyes, similar to having sand in them. The eyelids may become swollen and inflamed (blepharitis), and in severe cases, vision can be affected. Ocular rosacea often occurs in conjunction with other types of rosacea and requires prompt medical treatment to prevent complications. Regular eye examinations and proper eye hygiene are essential for managing this type.

5. Granulomatous Rosacea

This rare form of rosacea is characterized by hard, yellow, brown, or red nodules on the skin. These nodules are typically less inflamed than the papules and pustules seen in other types of rosacea. Granulomatous rosacea often affects the cheeks and around the eyes. The nodules can cause significant cosmetic concerns and may be challenging to treat.

This type requires specialized treatment and monitoring by a dermatologist.

Understanding the different types of rosacea can help individuals and healthcare providers identify the most appropriate treatment strategies. Early diagnosis and tailored treatment plans are crucial for managing the symptoms and preventing the progression of this chronic condition.

Symptoms of Rosacea

Rosacea manifests through a variety of symptoms, which can vary in severity from person to person. Here are some common symptoms:

- *Facial Redness:* Persistent redness, particularly in the central part of the face, is a hallmark of Rosacea. This redness can resemble a blush or sunburn that doesn't go away.
- *Visible Blood Vessels:* Small blood vessels on the nose and cheeks often become visible and more prominent.
- *Bumps and Pimples:* Many individuals with Rosacea develop small, red, pus-filled bumps that can be mistaken for acne.
- *Eye Irritation:* Rosacea can affect the eyes, causing them to feel dry, irritated, and swollen. This condition is known as ocular Rosacea.
- *Thickened Skin:* In some cases, Rosacea can cause the skin to thicken and enlarge, particularly around the

nose. This condition is called rhinophyma and is more common in men.
- *Burning or Stinging Sensations:* The affected skin may feel hot, tender, or painful.
- *Swelling:* Facial swelling, particularly around the eyes, can occur.

If you suspect you have Rosacea, it's important to consult a healthcare professional for a proper diagnosis and personalized treatment plan.

Causes of Rosacea

Rosacea is a chronic skin condition that causes redness and visible blood vessels in your face. While the exact cause of rosacea is unknown, several factors are believed to contribute to its development:

1. *Genetics:* A family history of rosacea can significantly increase your risk, suggesting that genetic factors may contribute to the condition's development. If your parents or siblings have experienced rosacea, you might be more susceptible to its symptoms.
2. *Immune System:* An overactive immune response may play a critical role in the onset of rosacea. This hyper-reactivity can cause the skin to become inflamed and sensitive, leading to the characteristic redness and bumps associated with the condition.

3. ***Environmental Triggers:*** Various environmental factors can exacerbate symptoms of rosacea. Sun exposure is a major trigger, as are extreme temperatures, whether hot or cold. Wind and high humidity levels can also irritate the skin, making it essential for those with rosacea to protect their skin from these elements.
4. ***Microorganisms:*** The presence of certain bacteria and mites, such as Demodex folliculorum, on the skin may contribute to the development of rosacea. These microorganisms can cause inflammation and disrupt the skin's natural barrier, leading to flare-ups.
5. ***Vascular Abnormalities:*** Issues with blood vessels in the face can lead to increased redness and flushing, common signs of rosacea. These vascular abnormalities may cause an enlarged appearance of blood vessels, making the skin look flushed or blotchy.
6. ***Diet and Lifestyle:*** Certain dietary choices and lifestyle habits can trigger flare-ups in individuals with rosacea. Spicy foods, alcohol, and hot beverages can dilate blood vessels and increase redness. Additionally, high stress levels can exacerbate symptoms, making stress management an important aspect of controlling the condition.
7. ***Hormonal Changes:*** Hormonal fluctuations, particularly in women, can influence the occurrence of rosacea. Changes during menstrual cycles, pregnancy,

or menopause can cause increased sensitivity and flare-ups, highlighting the importance of monitoring hormonal health in managing this condition.

Understanding these potential causes can help in managing and reducing the frequency of Rosacea flare-ups. If you suspect you have Rosacea, consulting a healthcare professional for a proper diagnosis and treatment plan is essential.

Medical Treatments for Rosacea

Medical treatments for Rosacea aim to manage symptoms and reduce flare-ups. Here are some common medical treatments:

1. **Topical Medications:** These medications are specifically formulated to be applied directly to the skin, targeting areas affected by rosacea to effectively reduce redness and inflammation. Common options include metronidazole, which has anti-inflammatory properties, azelaic acid, known for its ability to clear up skin and reduce swelling, and ivermectin, which can help alleviate symptoms by addressing certain skin mites associated with the condition.
2. **Oral Antibiotics:** For more severe cases of rosacea, dermatologists may prescribe oral antibiotics such as doxycycline and tetracycline. These medications work to reduce inflammation and inhibit bacterial growth, providing relief for those experiencing more intense

symptoms. It's crucial for patients to follow their healthcare provider's guidance regarding dosage and duration of treatment.

3. ***Oral Acne Drugs:*** In instances where other treatments prove ineffective, oral isotretinoin may be prescribed. This powerful medication is typically reserved for severe acne but has shown efficacy in treating rosacea as well. It works by reducing the size and activity of sebaceous glands, leading to a significant decrease in oil production and inflammation, making it a valuable option for managing stubborn cases.

4. ***Laser and Light Therapies:*** These advanced treatments utilize targeted technology to address visible blood vessels and reduce redness in the skin. Techniques such as intense pulsed light (IPL) and various laser therapies have become popular options for those seeking a more permanent solution. They work by delivering precise wavelengths of light that penetrate the skin, effectively shrinking blood vessels and promoting a more even skin tone.

5. ***Eye Drops and Oral Medications for Ocular Rosacea:*** If rosacea affects the eyes, resulting in discomfort or irritation, specific eye drops and oral medications can be prescribed to help manage symptoms. These treatments aim to reduce inflammation and protect the eyes from further

irritation, ensuring that individuals experiencing ocular rosacea can maintain comfort and visual health.

6. *Skin Care Products:* Dermatologists often recommend gentle skin care products that are free from irritants and harsh chemicals to help manage rosacea effectively. Look for products that are fragrance-free and non-comedogenic, as these are less likely to exacerbate symptoms. Incorporating soothing ingredients like aloe vera or chamomile can also promote healing and improve skin tolerance.

7. *Surgical Procedures:* In rare cases, when medical treatments have not provided sufficient relief, surgical options may be considered. Procedures such as electrosurgery or laser surgery can be utilized to remove thickened skin, particularly around the nose, which is a common manifestation of rosacea. These surgical interventions aim to improve both the appearance and comfort of individuals suffering from the condition.

Consulting a dermatologist is crucial for a personalized treatment plan, as they can recommend the most appropriate options based on the severity and type of Rosacea.

How to Diagnose Rosacea?

Diagnosing Rosacea typically involves a clinical evaluation by a healthcare professional, often a dermatologist. Here are the common steps involved in diagnosing Rosacea:

1. *Medical History:* The healthcare provider will start by taking a detailed medical history, including any symptoms, their duration, and any potential triggers. They may also ask about family history, as Rosacea can be hereditary.
2. *Physical Examination:* A thorough examination of the skin, particularly the face, will be conducted to look for common signs of Rosacea, such as redness, visible blood vessels, and bumps.
3. *Symptom Assessment:* The provider will assess the specific symptoms and their severity. This includes evaluating the presence of facial redness, pimples, eye irritation, and any thickening of the skin.
4. *Rule Out Other Conditions:* Since Rosacea can resemble other skin conditions like acne, eczema, or lupus, the healthcare provider may perform tests or ask questions to rule out these conditions.
5. *Ocular Examination:* If there are symptoms of eye irritation, an examination of the eyes may be conducted to check for ocular Rosacea.
6. *Skin Biopsy (Rarely):* In some cases, a skin biopsy may be performed to confirm the diagnosis. This

involves taking a small sample of skin for laboratory analysis.

Early diagnosis and treatment are essential for managing Rosacea effectively. If you suspect you have Rosacea, consulting a healthcare professional is the best course of action.

Natural Remedies for Treating Rosacea

While there is no known cure for Rosacea, it can be managed and controlled through proper treatment and self-care. There are also natural remedies that can help alleviate the symptoms of Rosacea, but it is important to consult with a healthcare professional before trying any new treatments. Here are some popular natural remedies for treating Rosacea:

- *Aloe Vera:* Renowned for its calming effects, aloe vera gel can be directly applied to the skin to alleviate redness and inflammation.
- *Chamomile:* Chamomile has anti-inflammatory properties. Using chamomile tea bags as a compress or applying chamomile cream can help soothe the skin.
- *Green Tea:* Green tea has antioxidant and anti-inflammatory properties. Applying cooled green tea to the skin or using green tea-based skincare products can help reduce redness.
- *Honey:* Raw honey, particularly Manuka honey, has antibacterial and anti-inflammatory properties.

Applying a thin layer to the affected area can help soothe the skin.
- *Oatmeal:* Colloidal oatmeal can help reduce itching and inflammation. An oatmeal mask or bath can provide relief for irritated skin.
- *Lavender Oil:* Diluted lavender essential oil can be applied to the skin to reduce inflammation and redness. Always perform a patch test first to ensure there's no allergic reaction.
- *Cucumber:* Cucumber slices or cucumber juice can be applied to the skin to provide a cooling effect and reduce redness.
- *Turmeric:* Turmeric has anti-inflammatory properties. A turmeric mask made with turmeric powder and yogurt or honey can help soothe the skin.
- *Licorice Extract:* Licorice root extract can help reduce redness and irritation. Look for skincare products containing licorice extract or apply a diluted solution to the skin.
- *Tea Tree Oil:* Diluted tea tree oil can help with inflammation and has antimicrobial properties. Use it sparingly and always dilute it with a carrier oil.

These natural remedies can complement medical treatments, but it's essential to consult with a healthcare professional before trying new treatments to ensure they are safe and suitable for your skin.

Managing Rosacea Through Diet

Rosacea, a chronic skin condition characterized by facial redness, visible blood vessels, and bumps, can be significantly influenced by diet. While the exact cause of Rosacea remains unknown, certain foods and beverages are known to trigger flare-ups and exacerbate symptoms.

Spicy foods, alcohol, and hot drinks are some common culprits that can lead to increased redness and inflammation. On the flip side, incorporating anti-inflammatory and soothing foods into your diet can help manage and reduce the frequency of Rosacea flare-ups.

Principles of The Rosacea Diet

Managing Rosacea through diet involves understanding and adhering to several key principles that can help minimize flare-ups and maintain healthy skin. Here are the fundamental principles of the Rosacea Diet:

1. ***Avoid Common Triggers:*** Certain foods and beverages are known to exacerbate Rosacea symptoms. Common culprits include spicy foods, alcohol, hot drinks, and

foods high in histamines like aged cheeses and cured meats. Identifying and eliminating these triggers from your diet can significantly reduce flare-ups.

2. ***Incorporate Anti-Inflammatory Foods:*** Foods rich in anti-inflammatory properties can help soothe the skin and reduce redness. Incorporate items like fatty fish (salmon, mackerel), leafy greens (spinach, kale), berries, nuts, and seeds. These foods can help combat inflammation from within.

3. ***Stay Hydrated:*** Adequate hydration is crucial for skin health. Drinking plenty of water throughout the day helps to maintain skin hydration and can potentially reduce the severity of Rosacea symptoms.

4. ***Monitor Individual Reactions:*** Rosacea triggers can vary from person to person. It's important to keep a food diary to track what you eat and how your skin reacts. This can help identify specific foods that may trigger your symptoms, allowing you to tailor your diet accordingly.

5. ***Maintain a Balanced Diet:*** A well-rounded diet that includes a variety of nutrients is essential for overall health and skin wellness. Ensure your diet is rich in vitamins, minerals, and antioxidants by including a wide range of fruits, vegetables, whole grains, and lean proteins.

6. ***Consult with a Healthcare Professional:*** Before making any significant dietary changes, it's essential to

consult with a healthcare professional or a registered dietitian. They can provide personalized advice and ensure that your diet meets your nutritional needs while effectively managing Rosacea.

By following these principles, individuals with Rosacea can take proactive steps to manage their condition and improve their skin health through thoughtful dietary choices.

Benefits of the Rosacea Diet

Adopting a diet tailored specifically for managing Rosacea can have a profound impact on your skin health and overall well-being. Here are some key benefits of following the Rosacea Diet:

1. ***Reduced Flare-Ups:*** One of the most significant advantages of the Rosacea Diet is the reduction in the frequency and severity of flare-ups. By avoiding common dietary triggers and incorporating anti-inflammatory foods, you can help keep your skin calm and minimize the occurrence of redness and irritation.
2. ***Improved Skin Appearance:*** A well-balanced diet rich in vitamins, minerals, and antioxidants can contribute to healthier skin. Following the Rosacea Diet can lead to a clearer, more even complexion, and a noticeable reduction in redness, visible blood vessels, and bumps.

3. ***Better Overall Skin Health:*** Proper nutrition is essential for maintaining skin integrity and resilience. The Rosacea Diet encourages the consumption of nutrient-dense foods that support skin repair and regeneration, leading to stronger and more resilient skin.
4. ***Enhanced Quality of Life:*** Living with Rosacea can be challenging, but managing it through diet can significantly improve your quality of life. Reduced symptoms mean less discomfort and self-consciousness, allowing you to engage more confidently in social and professional activities.
5. ***Complementary to Medical Treatments:*** While medical treatments are crucial for managing Rosacea, dietary changes can enhance their effectiveness. A well-planned diet can work synergistically with prescribed medications and topical treatments, providing a more comprehensive approach to managing the condition.
6. ***Long-Term Relief:*** Unlike some treatments that offer temporary relief, the benefits of the Rosacea Diet can be long-lasting. By consistently following dietary guidelines, you can achieve sustained improvements in your skin health and reduce the likelihood of future flare-ups.

By integrating the Rosacea Diet into your daily routine, you can take a proactive role in managing your condition, leading to healthier skin and a better overall sense of well-being.

Potential Drawbacks of the Rosacea Diet

While the Rosacea Diet offers numerous benefits, it's essential to be aware of some potential drawbacks that may arise when following this specialized dietary plan:

- *Dietary Restrictions:* Eliminating common triggers like spicy foods, alcohol, and certain dairy products can limit your dietary choices. This can make dining out or social gatherings where food is a central component more challenging.
- *Need for Careful Planning:* Following the Rosacea Diet requires meticulous planning and preparation. You may need to spend additional time researching recipes, meal prepping, and ensuring you have the right ingredients on hand, which can be time-consuming.
- *Potential Social Challenges:* Adhering to the Rosacea Diet in social settings can sometimes lead to awkward situations. You may need to explain your dietary restrictions to friends and family or decline certain foods and beverages, which can feel isolating.
- *Time to See Results:* Dietary changes often take a while to manifest in terms of improved skin health.

Patience is necessary, as it may take several weeks or even months to notice significant improvements in Rosacea symptoms.

Despite these disadvantages, the benefits of the Rosacea Diet far outweigh the drawbacks. The potential for reduced flare-ups, improved skin appearance, better overall skin health, enhanced quality of life, and long-term relief make it a worthwhile and effective approach to managing Rosacea.

Managing Rosacea Through Lifestyle Changes

Managing Rosacea effectively requires a comprehensive approach that goes beyond diet and medical treatments. Incorporating lifestyle changes can significantly help in reducing flare-ups and maintaining overall skin health. This chapter delves into various lifestyle modifications that can aid in managing Rosacea symptoms, including stress management, skincare routines, avoiding environmental triggers, and the importance of regular exercise.

Stress Management

Stress is a well-known trigger for Rosacea flare-ups. Learning to manage stress can help in reducing the frequency and severity of symptoms. Here are some practical tips for stress management:

- *Mindfulness and Meditation:* Practicing mindfulness and meditation can help reduce stress levels. Even a few minutes of deep breathing exercises daily can make a difference.

- *Yoga and Tai Chi:* These practices combine physical activity with stress reduction techniques, making them excellent options for managing stress.
- *Adequate Sleep:* Ensure you get enough restful sleep, as lack of sleep can exacerbate stress and trigger Rosacea symptoms.
- *Time Management:* Organize your daily activities to avoid unnecessary stress. Prioritize tasks and set realistic goals to prevent feeling overwhelmed.

Skincare Routines

A gentle and consistent skincare routine is crucial for managing Rosacea. The right products and techniques can soothe the skin and prevent flare-ups. Consider the following tips:

- *Gentle Cleansing:* Use a mild, fragrance-free cleanser to wash your face. Avoid scrubbing, as this can irritate the skin.
- *Moisturizing:* Apply a gentle, hypoallergenic moisturizer to keep your skin hydrated. Look for products containing ingredients like ceramides and hyaluronic acid.
- *Sun Protection:* Sun exposure can trigger Rosacea symptoms. Always apply a broad-spectrum sunscreen with at least SPF 30 before going outside. Choose a sunscreen formulated for sensitive skin.

- ***Avoid Harsh Products:*** Stay away from skincare products containing alcohol, menthol, and fragrances, as they can irritate the skin.

By following these tips and finding the right skincare routine, you can help manage your Rosacea and keep your skin healthy and happy. It's also essential to consult with a dermatologist for personalized recommendations and treatment options.

Avoiding Environmental Triggers

Environmental factors can also play a significant role in triggering Rosacea symptoms. Being mindful of these triggers and taking proactive steps can help manage the condition:

- ***Temperature Extremes:*** Avoid exposure to extreme temperatures. During hot weather, stay in air-conditioned environments, and during cold weather, protect your face with a scarf.
- ***Wind:*** Wind can irritate the skin. Use a protective barrier like a scarf or a hat to shield your face.
- ***Humidity:*** High humidity levels can cause sweating, which may aggravate Rosacea. Use fans or air conditioners to maintain a comfortable indoor climate.
- ***Pollution:*** Air pollutants can irritate sensitive skin. Try to avoid heavily polluted areas, and consider using air purifiers at home.

Importance of Regular Exercise

Regular physical activity is beneficial for overall health and well-being, but it can be challenging for individuals with Rosacea due to potential flare-ups caused by overheating and sweating. Here are some tips for managing exercise:

- *Low-Impact Activities:* Opt for low-impact exercises like walking, swimming, or cycling, which are less likely to cause overheating.
- *Cool Environments:* Exercise in a cool environment, such as an air-conditioned gym or during cooler times of the day, to prevent overheating.
- *Hydration:* Stay well-hydrated before, during, and after exercise to help regulate body temperature.
- *Clothing:* Wear breathable, moisture-wicking fabrics to keep sweat away from your skin.

Incorporating lifestyle changes into your daily routine can significantly enhance the management of Rosacea symptoms. Stress management, a gentle skincare routine, avoiding environmental triggers, and regular exercise are all vital components of a holistic approach to Rosacea care.

These modifications, when combined with dietary adjustments and medical treatments, provide a comprehensive strategy for maintaining healthier skin and improving the overall quality of life for individuals with Rosacea.

5-Step Plan to Get Started for Managing Rosacea Through Diet and Lifestyle Adjustments

Managing rosacea can be challenging, but with the right dietary and lifestyle adjustments, you can significantly reduce flare-ups and improve your skin's condition. Here's a 5-step plan to help you manage rosacea effectively:

Step 1: Identify and Avoid Trigger Foods

Certain foods and beverages can trigger rosacea flare-ups, making it essential to identify and avoid these triggers to manage the condition effectively. Common culprits include:

- *Spicy Foods:* Ingredients like chili peppers, hot sauce, and other spicy seasonings can cause blood vessels to dilate, leading to redness and irritation in individuals with rosacea.
- *Alcohol:* Especially red wine, is known to be a significant trigger for many people. The compounds in alcohol can increase blood flow to the skin, causing flare-ups. It's beneficial to limit or avoid alcohol

consumption entirely if you notice a correlation between drinking and rosacea symptoms.

- *Hot Beverages:* Consuming hot coffee, tea, or soup can lead to facial flushing due to the heat. Switching to iced or room-temperature drinks might help alleviate this issue.
- *Foods High in Histamines:* Certain foods, like aged cheeses, smoked meats, and fermented products (e.g., sauerkraut and soy sauce), are high in histamines and can provoke rosacea flare-ups. Fresh, unprocessed alternatives are generally better choices.

To effectively manage these dietary triggers:

Keep a Food Diary

Tracking everything you eat and drink daily is crucial for identifying rosacea triggers. Here's how to maintain an effective food diary:

- *Detail-Oriented Entries:* Make it a habit to note every meal, snack, and beverage you consume throughout the day, including all ingredients and their portion sizes. The more detailed your entries are, the easier it will be to identify potential triggers for any adverse reactions. For example, instead of just writing "salad," specify the types of greens, dressings, and any toppings, as each can play a role in your symptoms.

- *Timing:* Record the time of day you consume each item, as this can help you pinpoint not only what triggers flare-ups but also if there's a pattern related to timing. For instance, foods consumed later in the day might have a different impact than those eaten in the morning. You might notice that certain foods lead to flare-ups when eaten close to bedtime, allowing you to adjust your diet accordingly.
- *Symptoms Log:* Keep a detailed track of any skin reactions, such as redness, bumps, irritation, or other rosacea symptoms. Be meticulous about noting the onset, duration, and severity of these symptoms. Include any other factors that might contribute to these reactions, such as changes in weather or stress levels, which can also play a significant role in skin health.
- *Consistency:* Ensure that you make daily entries to build a comprehensive record over time. Consistency in logging your meals and symptoms helps to establish patterns and correlations that may not be apparent from sporadic entries. Aim to make this a daily routine, so it becomes a natural part of your day.
- *Review Regularly:* Take the time to periodically review your diary to look for trends or recurring triggers. This will not only help you in managing your symptoms but may also reveal insights that can lead to lifestyle adjustments. Sharing this diary with a healthcare professional can provide valuable insights

and help in developing a tailored approach for your condition. Regular reviews can also motivate you to stay committed to your tracking efforts.

Monitor Reactions

Paying close attention to your skin's reactions after consuming potential trigger foods is essential:

- *Immediate Reactions:* Begin by closely observing your skin within the first few hours after eating a particular food. Some foods, especially those known for common allergens such as nuts, shellfish, or dairy, may cause immediate redness or flushing, which can indicate a food sensitivity or allergy. It's important to document these reactions meticulously, as they can help identify specific triggers that may affect your skin.
- *Delayed Reactions:* Keep in mind that not all triggers cause instant reactions. Some foods may lead to skin flare-ups that manifest hours or even days after consumption. Therefore, it's wise to monitor your skin for up to 72 hours post-consumption. By doing so, you'll be able to capture any delayed responses, which may be crucial in understanding your body's unique reactions to various food items.
- *Severity and Type:* As you observe your skin, make careful notes regarding the severity of any reactions you experience, categorizing them as mild, moderate,

or severe. Additionally, take note of the type of reaction, which could include symptoms such as redness, bumps, itching, or even swelling. Keeping detailed records can significantly aid in distinguishing between different triggers and their effects over time, helping you to create a clearer picture of your skin's health.

- **Environmental Factors:** Lastly, consider other environmental variables that might influence your skin's responses. Factors such as fluctuations in weather (like humidity or temperature changes), stress levels, and the skincare products you apply on the same day can all impact your skin's condition. By taking these elements into account, you'll be in a better position to understand the full scope of what may be affecting your skin health and how to manage it effectively.

Elimination Diet

An elimination diet helps pinpoint specific foods that trigger rosacea symptoms:

- **Start with Basics:** Begin your journey by systematically eliminating common dietary triggers that may cause skin reactions, such as spicy foods, alcohol, hot beverages, and foods high in histamines like aged cheeses and cured meats. This initial step lays the foundation for identifying specific sensitivities.

- ***Remove One at a Time:*** After you've established a baseline by removing these foods, gradually reintroduce each eliminated item one by one. This methodical approach allows you to closely monitor your body's response to each food. Allow a few days between reintroductions to accurately assess any potential reactions, ensuring you give your body enough time to adjust.
- ***Document Changes:*** It's crucial to keep meticulous records of the foods you've removed and those you've reintroduced, along with any skin reactions you observe. Consider using a journal or a digital app to track this information, as it will help you identify patterns and make informed decisions moving forward.
- ***Be Patient:*** Understand that this process can be time-consuming, but it is highly effective in pinpointing specific triggers that may be affecting your skin. It's important to remain patient and adhere strictly to the elimination diet to achieve accurate results. Remember, the goal is to create a clearer picture of how different foods impact your skin.
- ***Balanced Nutrition:*** While eliminating certain foods, it's essential to ensure you continue to maintain a balanced and nutritious diet. Explore alternative options rich in vitamins and minerals to meet your

nutritional needs, such as incorporating more fruits, vegetables, and whole grains. This way, you can support your overall health while identifying potential triggers.

Consult a Nutritionist or Dermatologist

Professional advice can significantly enhance your management strategy:

- ***Personalized Guidance:*** A qualified nutritionist can work closely with you to create a highly tailored diet plan that specifically avoids common dietary triggers while ensuring that your nutritional needs are fully met. They possess the expertise to suggest safe and beneficial food substitutes that not only mitigate symptoms but also support overall health and wellness, allowing you to enjoy a varied and satisfying diet.
- ***Medical Evaluation:*** A licensed dermatologist will conduct a thorough assessment of your skin condition, providing expert treatments designed to manage your symptoms effectively. They can recommend skincare products that are gentle and non-irritating, ensuring that you maintain a healthy complexion while minimizing flare-ups. Their insights into your skin type and specific concerns will be invaluable in developing a personalized skincare routine.
- ***Support and Monitoring:*** Professionals in this field offer ongoing support and can monitor your progress

over time. They will review your food diary and symptom log regularly to assess your response to dietary changes and treatments. This collaborative approach allows them to adjust recommendations and strategies as needed, optimizing your management plan and empowering you to take control of your health journey.

- ***Education and Resources:*** Both nutritionists and dermatologists play a crucial role in educating you about rosacea, helping you gain a deeper understanding of this condition. They provide valuable resources and insights, empowering you to make informed decisions regarding your lifestyle and diet. This knowledge not only aids in effective management but also fosters a sense of confidence as you navigate your health challenges.

Step 2: Incorporate Anti-Inflammatory Foods

A diet rich in anti-inflammatory foods can help reduce overall inflammation and alleviate rosacea symptoms. By focusing on nutrient-dense, anti-inflammatory options, you can support skin health and minimize flare-ups. Here's a deeper dive into incorporating these beneficial foods:

1. **Omega-3 Fatty Acids**

   Omega-3 fatty acids are renowned for their powerful anti-inflammatory properties. They help to reduce inflammation at the cellular level, which can be particularly beneficial for managing rosacea.

   - *Fish:* Fatty fish like salmon, mackerel, sardines, and trout are excellent sources of omega-3s. Aim to include these in your diet at least two times per week.
   - *Plant-Based Sources:* If you prefer plant-based options, flaxseeds, chia seeds, and walnuts are great alternatives. Ground flaxseeds can be added to smoothies, yogurts, or oatmeal, while chia seeds can be used to make chia pudding or sprinkled on salads.

2. **Fruits and Vegetables**

   Fruits and vegetables are rich in antioxidants, vitamins, and minerals that combat inflammation and promote overall skin health.

   - *Berries:* Blueberries, strawberries, raspberries, and blackberries are packed with antioxidants like vitamin C and flavonoids, which help protect the skin from oxidative stress.
   - *Leafy Greens:* Spinach, kale, Swiss chard, and collard greens are high in vitamins A, C, and K, as well as anti-inflammatory compounds.

Include a variety of greens in salads, smoothies, or sautéed dishes.

- ***Bell Peppers:*** All colors of bell peppers are excellent sources of vitamin C and beta-carotene, which can help reduce inflammation. They can be eaten raw, roasted, or added to stir-fries.

3. Whole Grains

Whole grains provide fiber, vitamins, and minerals that support digestive health and reduce inflammation.

- ***Quinoa:*** A versatile grain that is high in protein and fiber, quinoa can be used in salads, bowls, or as a side dish.
- ***Brown Rice:*** Rich in magnesium and fiber, brown rice is a healthier alternative to refined grains. It can be paired with vegetables, and proteins, or used in soups.
- ***Oatmeal:*** Oats are a great source of soluble fiber, which can help manage blood sugar levels and reduce inflammation. Enjoy oatmeal for breakfast with fruits and nuts for added nutrients.

4. Turmeric and Ginger

Both turmeric and ginger have been used for centuries in traditional medicine for their anti-inflammatory and antioxidant properties.

- ***Turmeric:*** Curcumin, the active compound in turmeric, has strong anti-inflammatory effects. Add turmeric to soups, stews, curries, or smoothies. Combining it with black pepper enhances its absorption.
- ***Ginger:*** Ginger contains gingerol, which has potent anti-inflammatory and antioxidant effects. Fresh ginger can be added to teas, stir-fries, and smoothies, or used in marinades and dressings.

Practical Tips for Incorporation

- ***Meal Planning:*** Plan your meals around these anti-inflammatory foods. Create a weekly menu that includes a variety of fruits, vegetables, whole grains, and omega-3-rich foods.
- ***Cooking Methods:*** Opt for cooking methods that preserve the nutrients and enhance the anti-inflammatory properties of these foods, such as steaming, roasting, grilling, and sautéing.
- ***Snacks:*** Keep healthy snacks like berries, nuts, and seed mixes on hand for easy access throughout the day.
- ***Smoothies:*** Blend leafy greens, berries, flaxseeds, and a piece of ginger into a smoothie for a nutrient-packed start to your day.

By consistently incorporating these anti-inflammatory foods into your diet, you can help reduce the overall inflammation in your body, thereby managing rosacea symptoms more effectively. Always consult with a healthcare professional before making significant dietary changes, especially if you have any underlying health conditions.

Step 3: Stay Hydrated

Proper hydration is essential for maintaining skin health and managing rosacea. Adequate water intake helps keep your skin hydrated, reduces dryness, and can minimize flare-ups.

Here's a more detailed look at how staying hydrated can benefit your skin and tips on how to achieve optimal hydration:

Importance of Hydration

- *Skin Moisture:* Water plays a crucial role in maintaining the skin's moisture balance, acting as a natural hydrator. When skin is well-hydrated, it is less likely to become dry, flaky, and irritated. This is particularly important for individuals with skin conditions like rosacea, as adequate moisture can help mitigate flare-ups and alleviate symptoms, leading to a healthier complexion overall.
- *Toxin Removal:* Drinking plenty of water is essential for flushing out toxins from your body, a process that supports overall health. By staying hydrated, you promote efficient kidney function, which helps eliminate waste products and reduces the burden on

your skin. This detoxification process can lead to decreased inflammation, paving the way for clearer skin and a more vibrant appearance.

- ***Cellular Function:*** Proper hydration is vital for overall cellular function, as water is a key component in various biological processes. Staying well-hydrated ensures that skin cells receive the essential nutrients they need to repair and regenerate effectively. This not only aids in maintaining skin elasticity and firmness but also contributes to a radiant glow, highlighting the importance of water in your skincare routine.

Tips for Staying Hydrated

1. *Daily Water Intake*

   Aim to drink at least 8 glasses (64 ounces) of water per day. This recommendation serves as a general guideline; however, individual needs can vary significantly based on factors such as your activity level, the climate you live in, and even your overall health. For instance, if you are exercising vigorously or spending time in hot weather, you may need to increase your intake to stay adequately hydrated.

2. *Consistent Hydration*

   It's important to spread your water intake throughout the day rather than consuming large amounts at once. This approach not only helps maintain consistent hydration but also allows your body to absorb the water more effectively. Consider setting reminders on your phone or using a marked water bottle to encourage regular sipping throughout the day.

3. *Hydrating Foods*

Boost your hydration by adding water-rich foods to your diet. Excellent options include cucumbers, watermelons, oranges, strawberries, and leafy greens. These foods not only keep you hydrated but also supply vital vitamins and minerals essential for overall health. Incorporating a range of these foods into your meals can help you stay hydrated while enjoying tasty and nutritious flavors.

4. *Infused Water*

If plain water feels monotonous or unappealing, consider infusing it with slices of fruits, vegetables, or herbs to enhance its flavor. Options like lemon, cucumber, mint, or berries can transform your water into a refreshing beverage without adding any extra calories or sugars. Experimenting with different combinations can make staying hydrated much more enjoyable and can also provide additional nutrients.

5. *Track Your Intake*

Keeping track of your water consumption can be a helpful way to ensure you are meeting your daily hydration goals. Use a water bottle with measurements marked on the side, or consider downloading a hydration tracking app that allows you to monitor your intake throughout the day. By regularly checking in on your hydration habits, you can make adjustments as needed to maintain optimal hydration levels for your health and well-being.

Avoid Dehydration Triggers

- *Caffeinated Drinks:* While moderate caffeine consumption is generally okay, excessive intake of caffeinated beverages like coffee, tea, and soda can lead to dehydration. Caffeine is a diuretic, which means it can increase urine production and result in fluid loss. Balance caffeinated drinks with extra water intake.
- *Alcohol:* Alcohol can also dehydrate your body. If you consume alcohol, make sure to drink water alongside it to stay hydrated.
- *Sugary Beverages:* Drinks high in sugar, such as sodas and sweetened fruit juices, can contribute to inflammation and are best consumed in moderation. Opt for natural, unsweetened alternatives whenever possible.

Hydration and Skincare

- *Moisturizing from the Inside Out:* While topical moisturizers are important, hydrating from within is equally crucial. Drinking enough water helps maintain the skin's elasticity and suppleness.
- *Skincare Products:* Complement your hydration efforts with a good skincare routine. Use hydrating serums, creams, and masks that contain ingredients like hyaluronic acid, glycerin, and aloe vera that help attract and retain moisture in the skin.

By prioritizing proper hydration, you can support your skin's health and potentially reduce the severity and frequency of rosacea flare-ups. Remember that individual hydration needs can vary, so it's important to listen to your body and adjust your water intake accordingly.

Step 4: Adopt a Gentle Skincare Routine

Your skincare routine plays a crucial role in managing rosacea. It's important to use products that are gentle on the skin, avoid potential irritants, and focus on hydration and protection. Here's an expanded guide to adopting a gentle skincare routine:

Use Gentle, Hypoallergenic Products

- *Avoid Irritants:* Choose skincare products that are free from alcohol, fragrances, essential oils, and harsh

chemicals, as these ingredients can irritate sensitive skin and exacerbate rosacea symptoms.
- *Hypoallergenic Options:* Opt for products labeled as hypoallergenic or designed for sensitive skin. These are formulated to minimize the risk of allergic reactions and irritation.
- *Patch Test:* Always perform a patch test before introducing a new product into your routine. Apply a small amount to a discreet area of your skin and wait 24-48 hours to check for any adverse reactions.
- *Gentle Cleansers:* Use a mild, non-foaming cleanser to remove dirt and makeup without stripping your skin of its natural oils. Look for cleansers with soothing ingredients like chamomile, aloe vera, or cucumber extract.

Moisturize Regularly

- *Non-Comedogenic Hydrators:* Choose non-comedogenic (won't clog pores), hydrating moisturizers that help strengthen the skin barrier. Ingredients like hyaluronic acid, glycerin, and ceramides are excellent for retaining moisture.
- *Barrier Repair:* Moisturizers that focus on repairing and maintaining the skin barrier can help reduce sensitivity and prevent moisture loss. Look for products with niacinamide or panthenol, which support skin barrier function.

- *Consistency:* Apply moisturizer at least twice daily, in the morning and evening. This helps keep the skin hydrated throughout the day and overnight.
- *Layering:* In colder or drier climates, consider layering a hydrating serum under your moisturizer for added moisture retention.

Sun Protection

1. Daily Sunscreen

It's crucial to wear sunscreen every single day, even on overcast days or when spending time indoors, with a minimum SPF of 30. Remember that UV rays can penetrate clouds and windows, and consistent sun exposure can exacerbate conditions like rosacea, leading to uncomfortable flare-ups and skin irritation.

2. Physical (Mineral) Sunscreens

When choosing a sunscreen, it's advisable to opt for physical (mineral) formulations that contain zinc oxide or titanium dioxide. These ingredients sit on the skin's surface and reflect UV rays, making them a safer choice for those with sensitive skin, as they are less likely to cause irritation compared to their chemical counterparts, which can sometimes lead to allergic reactions.

3. Broad-Spectrum Protection

Always ensure that your sunscreen provides broad-spectrum protection. This means it effectively shields your skin from both UVA rays, which can prematurely age the skin, and UVB rays, which are primarily responsible for sunburn. Look for labels that specify "broad-spectrum" to guarantee comprehensive defense against harmful sun exposure.

4. Reapplication

For optimal protection, remember to reapply sunscreen every two hours while outdoors. If you're swimming or sweating heavily, it's essential to reapply immediately afterward, as even water-resistant formulas can lose effectiveness when exposed to moisture.

Additional Protective Measures

To further enhance your sun protection strategy, complement sunscreen use with physical barriers. Wearing wide-brimmed hats can shield your face and neck, while sunglasses with UV protection can safeguard your eyes from harmful rays. Additionally, seeking shade during peak sun hours, typically between 10 a.m. and 4 p.m., can significantly reduce your risk of sun damage. These combined efforts will help keep your skin healthy and protected all year round.

Additional Skincare Tips

- *Cool Water:* It's best to wash your face with lukewarm or cool water instead of hot water, which can aggravate rosacea and lead to increased redness and irritation. Cool water is gentler on the skin and helps maintain your skin's natural moisture barrier.
- *Minimalist Approach:* Keeping your skincare routine simple is vital for sensitive skin. Using too many products can overwhelm and irritate the skin, leading to breakouts or flare-ups. Focus on a basic regimen that prioritizes cleansing, moisturizing, and sun protection to maintain healthy, balanced skin.
- *Avoid Scrubs and Exfoliants:* Physical exfoliants and harsh scrubbing can be detrimental to sensitive skin, causing further irritation and inflammation. If you feel the need to exfoliate, opt for a gentle chemical exfoliant like lactic acid, which is milder and can help remove dead skin cells without causing redness. Remember to use it sparingly to avoid disrupting your skin's natural barrier.
- *Soothing Treatments:* Incorporate calming treatments into your routine that contain anti-inflammatory ingredients, such as green tea extract, licorice root, or Centella Asiatica (cica). These ingredients can help soothe redness and inflammation, providing relief and promoting a more even skin tone. Regular use of these

treatments can enhance your skin's resilience against irritation.

By adopting a gentle skincare routine tailored to your skin's needs, you can effectively manage rosacea symptoms and maintain healthier, more resilient skin.

Step 5: Manage Stress

Stress is a well-known trigger for rosacea, and effectively managing it can significantly improve your skin's condition and overall well-being. Here's a deeper look at incorporating stress-reducing practices into your daily routine:

1. **Mindfulness and Meditation**
   - *Regular Practice:* Incorporate mindfulness and meditation into your daily routine. Start with short sessions of 5-10 minutes and gradually increase the duration as you get more comfortable.
   - *Techniques:* Practice techniques such as focused breathing, body scans, and guided imagery to help calm the mind and reduce stress.
   - *Apps and Resources:* Use meditation apps like Headspace, Calm, or Insight Timer for guided sessions and mindfulness exercises.

- ***Consistency:*** Make meditation a regular part of your day, whether it's in the morning to set a positive tone or in the evening to unwind.

2. **Exercise**
   - ***Moderate Physical Activities:*** Engage in moderate activities like yoga, walking, or swimming, which can help reduce stress without causing overheating—a potential trigger for rosacea.
   - ***Routine:*** Aim for at least 30 minutes of physical activity most days of the week. This can be broken down into shorter sessions if needed.
   - ***Mind-Body Exercises:*** Yoga and tai chi are excellent options as they combine physical movement with breathing exercises and mindfulness, promoting relaxation and stress relief.
   - ***Outdoor Activities:*** Spending time in nature can further enhance the stress-reducing benefits of exercise. Go for walks in parks, hike on trails, or swim in natural bodies of water when possible.

3. **Adequate Sleep**
   - ***Sleep Hygiene:*** Establish a regular sleep schedule by going to bed and waking up at the same time each day, even on weekends. This

helps regulate your body's internal clock and improve sleep quality.
- **Relaxing Bedtime Routine:** Create a calming pre-sleep routine that includes activities like reading, listening to soothing music, or taking a warm bath. Avoid stimulating activities and screens at least an hour before bed.
- **Comfortable Sleep Environment:** Ensure your bedroom is conducive to sleep by keeping it cool, dark, and quiet. Invest in a comfortable mattress and pillows and minimize noise disruptions.
- **Limit Stimulants:** Avoid caffeine and heavy meals close to bedtime, as they can interfere with your ability to fall asleep and stay asleep.

Additional Stress-Reducing Practices

- Time Management: Organize your day to include breaks and avoid overloading yourself with tasks. Prioritize activities that contribute to your well-being.
- Hobbies and Interests: Engage in activities you enjoy and that bring you joy, whether it's reading, gardening, painting, or playing a musical instrument. Hobbies can provide a mental break and reduce stress.
- Social Support: Spend time with friends and family who provide emotional support. Talking about your

- Professional Help: If stress becomes overwhelming, consider seeking help from a mental health professional. Therapists and counselors can provide strategies and support tailored to your needs.

experiences and feelings with loved ones can help alleviate stress.

Implementing these stress-reducing steps can significantly help manage rosacea and improve your overall skin health. By taking a holistic approach to stress management, you can create a balanced lifestyle that supports both your mental and physical well-being.

Always consult with a healthcare professional or a dermatologist before making significant changes to your diet, skincare routine, or lifestyle.

Foods to Eat

Incorporating certain foods into your diet can help manage rosacea symptoms by reducing inflammation and supporting overall skin health. Here are some beneficial foods to include in a rosacea-friendly diet:

1. **Omega-3 Rich Foods**
    - *Fatty Fish:* Salmon, mackerel, sardines, trout, and herring
    - *Plant-Based Sources:* Flaxseeds, chia seeds, walnuts, and hemp seeds

2. **Anti-Inflammatory Fruits and Vegetables**
   - *Berries:* Blueberries, strawberries, raspberries, and blackberries
   - *Leafy Greens:* Spinach, kale, Swiss chard, and collard greens
   - *Cruciferous Vegetables:* Broccoli, cauliflower, Brussels sprouts, and cabbage
   - *Colorful Vegetables:* Bell peppers, carrots, sweet potatoes, and beets
   - *Fruits:* Apples, pears, peaches, and cherries
3. **Whole Grains**
   - *Quinoa:* A high-protein, fiber-rich grain
   - *Brown Rice:* A nutritious alternative to refined grains
   - *Oatmeal:* A great source of soluble fiber
4. **Herbs and Spices**
   - *Turmeric:* Contains curcumin, known for its anti-inflammatory properties
   - *Ginger:* Contains gingerol, which has potent anti-inflammatory effects
5. **Healthy Fats**
   - *Avocados:* Rich in healthy monounsaturated fats and antioxidants
   - *Olive Oil:* A staple in anti-inflammatory diets, rich in oleic acid
   - *Nuts and Seeds:* Almonds, sunflower seeds, and pumpkin seeds

6. **Hydrating Foods**
    - *Cucumbers:* High water content and soothing properties
    - *Watermelon:* Hydrating and packed with antioxidants
    - *Citrus Fruits:* Oranges, lemons, and grapefruits, which provide vitamin C
7. **Fermented Foods**
    - *Yogurt:* Contains probiotics that support gut health
    - *Kefir:* A fermented dairy product rich in probiotics
    - *Sauerkraut and Kimchi:* Fermented vegetables that support a healthy gut microbiome
8. **Beverages**
    - *Green Tea:* Rich in antioxidants and polyphenols
    - *Chamomile Tea:* Known for its calming and anti-inflammatory effects
    - *Water:* Essential for maintaining hydration and flushing out toxins

Incorporating these foods into your diet can help reduce inflammation, support skin health, and manage rosacea symptoms more effectively. Remember to consult with a healthcare professional or a nutritionist before making significant dietary changes.

Foods to Avoid

Certain foods and beverages can trigger or exacerbate rosacea symptoms. Avoiding these can help manage flare-ups and maintain healthier skin. Here are common foods to avoid if you have rosacea:

1. **Spicy Foods**
    - *Hot Peppers:* Jalapeños, habaneros, and other spicy varieties
    - *Spicy Sauces:* Hot sauce, salsa, and spicy curries
    - *Spices:* Cayenne pepper, chili powder, and paprika
2. **Alcoholic Beverages**
    - *Red Wine:* Known to be a significant trigger for many people with rosacea
    - *Other Alcohol:* Beer, whiskey, vodka, and other spirits
3. **Hot Beverages**
    - *Hot Coffee:* Can cause flushing and trigger rosacea symptoms
    - *Hot Tea:* Including black tea, green tea, and herbal teas served hot
    - *Hot Chocolate:* Especially due to the combination of heat and dairy

4. **Dairy Products**
   - *Milk:* Whole milk, skim milk, and flavored milk
   - *Cheese:* Aged cheeses such as cheddar, blue cheese, and gouda
   - *Yogurt:* Especially full-fat or flavored varieties
5. **Processed and High-Sugar Foods**
   - *Fast Food:* Burgers, fries, and fried chicken
   - *Sweets and Desserts:* Cakes, cookies, ice cream, and candies
   - *Sugary Drinks:* Sodas, sweetened teas, and fruit juices with added sugars
6. **Histamine-Rich Foods**
   - *Aged and Fermented Foods:* Sauerkraut, soy sauce, miso, and fermented sausages
   - *Canned and Processed Meats:* Bacon, ham, and deli meats
   - *Certain Vegetables:* Spinach, eggplant, and tomatoes
7. **Certain Fruits and Vegetables**
   - *Citrus Fruits:* Oranges, lemons, limes, and grapefruits
   - *Tomatoes:* Including tomato-based products like sauces and soups
   - *Avocados:* For some individuals sensitive to high histamine foods

8. **Foods with Additives**
    - *Artificial Sweeteners:* Aspartame, saccharin, and sucralose
    - *Preservatives:* Sodium benzoate, nitrates, and sulfites
    - *Colorants and Flavorings:* Artificial colors and flavors

Avoiding these potential triggers can help you better manage rosacea symptoms and reduce the frequency and severity of flare-ups. It's important to note that individual triggers may vary, so keeping a detailed food diary can help identify personal sensitivities.

7-Day Sample Meal Plan

We understand that navigating a new dietary plan can be overwhelming, which is why we have created a 7-day sample meal plan to help guide you. Keep in mind that this is just a general example and it's important to listen to your body and make adjustments as needed. Here's a balanced and varied meal plan designed to help manage rosacea symptoms by focusing on anti-inflammatory, nutrient-rich foods while avoiding common triggers.

Day 1

Breakfast

- Oatmeal with Blueberries and Chia Seeds

Lunch

- Quinoa salad with spinach, cucumber, bell peppers,
- Grilled salmon

Snack:

- Apple slices with almond butter

Dinner: Baked chicken breast with steamed broccoli and brown rice

Dessert: Fresh strawberries

Day 2

Breakfast: Smoothie with spinach, banana, flaxseeds, and water

Lunch: Turkey and avocado wrap in a whole-grain tortilla with a side of mixed greens

Snack: Carrot sticks with hummus

Dinner: Grilled shrimp with quinoa and roasted Brussels sprouts

Dessert: Sliced peaches

Day 3

Breakfast: Greek yogurt (plain) with honey and sliced almonds

Lunch: Lentil soup with a side of mixed green salad

Snack: Celery sticks with sunflower seed butter

Dinner: Baked cod with sweet potato mash and sautéed kale

Dessert: Pear slices

Day 4

Breakfast: Scrambled eggs with spinach and a side of whole-grain toast

Lunch: Chickpea salad with cherry tomatoes, cucumbers, olives, and olive oil dressing

Snack: Handful of walnuts

Dinner: Turkey meatballs with zucchini noodles and marinara sauce (tomato-free if sensitive)

Dessert: Fresh raspberries

Day 5

Breakfast: Buckwheat pancakes with a drizzle of maple syrup and fresh berries

Lunch: Grilled chicken Caesar salad with a light vinaigrette

Snack: Sliced bell peppers with guacamole

Dinner: Stir-fried tofu with mixed vegetables (broccoli, bell peppers, carrots) and brown rice

Dessert: Kiwi slices

Day 6

Breakfast: Chia pudding made with almond milk, topped with fresh mango

Lunch: Tuna salad with mixed greens, cucumbers, and olive oil dressing

Snack: A handful of pumpkin seeds

Dinner: Baked salmon with quinoa and a side of roasted asparagus

Dessert: Sliced melon

Day 7

Breakfast: Smoothie bowl with banana, spinach, avocado, and topped with sunflower seeds

Lunch: Grilled chicken and vegetable kebabs (zucchini, bell peppers, onions) with a side of quinoa

Snack: Fresh cherry tomatoes with a sprinkle of sea salt

Dinner: Lentil stew with carrots, celery, and sweet potatoes

Dessert: Apple slices with cinnamon

This 7-day meal plan for a rosacea diet is designed to help manage symptoms by incorporating anti-inflammatory and nutrient-rich foods while avoiding common triggers. By following this balanced and varied plan, you can support your overall skin health and reduce the frequency and severity of rosacea flare-ups.

Remember to stay hydrated, eat mindfully, and prepare meals in advance to ensure consistency in your diet. Always consult with a healthcare professional or a dermatologist before making significant dietary changes to tailor the plan to your specific needs. Adopting these dietary habits can contribute to clearer, healthier skin and improved well-being.

Sample Recipes

In chapter 5, we discussed the importance of following a balanced and varied diet to help manage rosacea symptoms. This chapter will provide some sample recipes that are suitable for a rosacea diet.

Oatmeal with Blueberries and Chia Seeds

Ingredients:

- 1 cup of rolled oats
- 1 cup of almond milk (or any non-dairy milk)
- 1/2 cup of fresh blueberries
- 1 tbsp of chia seeds
- Optional toppings: sliced almonds, honey, or maple syrup for sweetness

Instructions:

1. In a small saucepan, bring almond milk to a boil.
2. Add rolled oats and reduce heat to low. Cook for about 5 minutes, stirring occasionally.
3. Once the oatmeal thickens, remove it from the heat and let it cool for a few minutes.
4. Top with fresh blueberries and chia seeds.
5. Optional: add sliced almonds or drizzle honey/maple syrup on top for added flavor.
6. Enjoy this nutritious and filling breakfast!

Quinoa Salad

Ingredients:

- 1 cup of cooked quinoa
- 1 cup of fresh spinach leaves
- 1/2 cucumber, chopped
- 1 bell pepper, chopped (any color)
- 4 oz tofu, cubed
- Dressing: 2 tbsp olive oil, 1 tbsp apple cider vinegar, salt and pepper to taste.

Instructions:

1. Cook quinoa according to package instructions and let it cool.
2. In a large mixing bowl, combine cooked quinoa with spinach leaves, cucumber, bell pepper, and tofu.
3. In a separate small bowl, whisk together olive oil and apple cider vinegar for dressing. Add salt and pepper to taste.
4. Pour dressing over quinoa salad and mix well.
5. This salad can be served immediately or refrigerated for later use.

Grilled Salmon with Roasted Vegetables

Ingredients:

- 4 salmon fillets
- 1 bunch of asparagus
- 1 zucchini, sliced
- 1 red bell pepper, chopped
- 2 cloves of garlic, minced
- Juice of 1 lemon
- Salt and pepper to taste

Instructions:

1. Preheat grill to medium-high heat.
2. In a large bowl, mix together asparagus, zucchini, bell pepper, garlic, lemon juice, salt and pepper.
3. Place salmon fillets on top of the vegetable mixture.
4. Grill salmon and vegetables for about 10 minutes or until fish is cooked through.
5. Serve hot and enjoy this healthy and flavorful meal!

Baked Chicken Breast with Steamed Broccoli

Ingredients:

- 4 boneless chicken breasts
- 1 tsp garlic powder
- 1 tsp onion powder
- Salt and pepper to taste
- 2 tbsp olive oil

For the broccoli:

- 1 head of broccoli, cut into florets
- 2 tbsp water

Instructions:

1. Preheat oven to 375°F.
2. Season chicken breasts with garlic powder, onion powder, salt, and pepper on both sides.
3. Heat olive oil in a large skillet over medium heat.
4. Add chicken breasts to the skillet and cook for about 5 minutes on each side until golden brown.
5. Transfer chicken to a baking dish and bake in the oven for 20 minutes or until cooked through.
6. In a separate pot, steam broccoli with water for about 5 minutes until tender.
7. Serve chicken and steamed broccoli together as a healthy and satisfying meal option.

Turkey and Avocado Wrap

Ingredients:

- 4 whole wheat tortillas
- 1 lb deli turkey slices
- 1 avocado, sliced
- 4 leaves of lettuce
- 1 tomato, sliced

For the spread:

- ½ cup plain Greek yogurt
- Juice of ½ a lemon
- Salt and pepper to taste

Instructions:

1. In a small bowl, mix together Greek yogurt, lemon juice, salt, and pepper to make the spread.
2. Lay out tortillas on a flat surface.
3. Spread the Greek yogurt mixture on each tortilla.
4. Place a leaf of lettuce on top of the spread on each tortilla.
5. Layer turkey slices on top of the lettuce.
6. Add slices of avocado and tomato on top of the turkey.
7. Roll up each tortilla tightly to create a wrap.
8. Serve as is or cut in half for easier handling.

Grilled Shrimp with Quinoa

Ingredients:

- 1 lb shrimp, peeled and deveined
- 2 tbsp olive oil
- Salt and pepper to taste

For the quinoa:

- 1 cup quinoa
- 2 cups water

For the marinade:

- Juice of ½ a lemon
- 2 cloves of garlic, minced
- ¼ cup olive oil
- Salt and pepper to taste

Instructions:

1. In a small bowl, whisk together lemon juice, minced garlic, olive oil, salt, and pepper to create the marinade.
2. Place shrimp in a large resealable bag and pour marinade over them. Let marinate for at least 30 minutes.
3. In a small pot, add quinoa and water and bring to a boil. Reduce heat and let simmer for about 15 minutes or until all the water is absorbed.

4. Heat olive oil on a grill pan or outdoor grill over medium-high heat.
5. Season marinated shrimp with salt and pepper before placing them on the grill.
6. Grill shrimp for about 2-3 minutes on each side, until cooked through and slightly charred.
7. Serve grilled shrimp over cooked quinoa as a healthy and flavorful meal option.

Lentil Soup with a Side of Mixed Green Salad

Ingredients:

- 1 cup dried lentils, rinsed and drained
- 4 cups vegetable broth
- 2 cloves of garlic, minced
- 1 onion, chopped
- 1 carrot, chopped
- 2 stalks of celery, chopped
- Salt and pepper to taste

For the mixed green salad:

- Mixed greens (spinach, kale, arugula)
- Cherry tomatoes, halved
- Cucumber slices

For the dressing:

- Juice of ½ a lemon
- 2 tbsp olive oil
- Salt and pepper to taste

Instructions:

1. In a large pot, sauté garlic and onions in olive oil until fragrant.
2. Add in chopped carrots and celery, cooking until slightly softened.
3. Pour in vegetable broth and bring to a boil.

4. Stir in lentils and let simmer for about 20-25 minutes, until lentils are tender but not mushy.
5. Season with salt and pepper to taste before serving hot.
6. For the mixed green salad, toss together your choice of mixed greens with cherry tomatoes, cucumber slices, and any other desired toppings like avocado or croutons.
7. In a small bowl, whisk together lemon juice, olive oil, salt and pepper to create a simple dressing for the salad.
8. Serve the lentil soup with a side of mixed green salad and enjoy a satisfying and nutritious meal.

Baked Cod with Sweet Potato Mash and Sautéed Kale

Ingredients:

- 4 fresh cod fillets
- Salt and pepper to taste
- 2 sweet potatoes, peeled and chopped
- 1 tbsp olive oil

For the sautéed kale:

- 1 bunch of kale, stems removed and chopped into bite-sized pieces
- 2 cloves of garlic, minced
- 1 tbsp olive oil

For the honey mustard glaze:

- 1 tbsp Dijon mustard
- 1 tbsp honey

Instructions:

1. Preheat oven to 400 degrees F (200 degrees C).
2. Season cod fillets with salt and pepper on both sides.
3. In a large baking dish, lightly coat the bottom with olive oil.
4. Place cod fillets in the dish and bake for 15 minutes, or until fish is flaky and cooked through.

5. While the cod is cooking, boil sweet potatoes in a pot of water until tender.
6. Drain the sweet potatoes and mash with a fork or potato masher until smooth.
7. For the sautéed kale, heat olive oil in a pan over medium-high heat.
8. Add minced garlic and cook for about 1 minute, until fragrant.
9. Add chopped kale and sauté for 5-7 minutes, until wilted and slightly crispy.
10. In a small bowl, mix together Dijon mustard and honey to create the glaze.
11. Once the cod is done baking, remove from oven and brush with the honey mustard glaze.
12. Serve the baked cod with a side of sweet potato mash and sautéed kale for a delicious, balanced meal packed with protein and nutrients.

Turkey Meatballs with Zucchini Noodles

Ingredients:

- 1 lb ground turkey
- 1 egg
- ¼ cup breadcrumbs
- 2 cloves of garlic, minced
- ½ tsp salt
- ½ tsp pepper

For the zucchini noodles:

- 4 large zucchinis, spiralized or cut into thin strips
- 1 tbsp olive oil

For the marinara sauce:

- 1 can diced tomatoes
- 2 cloves of garlic, minced
- 1 tbsp olive oil

Instructions:

1. Preheat oven to 375 degrees F (190 degrees C).
2. In a large bowl, mix together ground turkey, egg, breadcrumbs, minced garlic, salt and pepper until well combined.
3. Roll the mixture into small meatballs, about 1 inch in diameter.

4. Place the meatballs on a baking sheet lined with parchment paper.
5. Bake for 20-25 minutes, or until cooked through and no longer pink in the middle.
6. While the meatballs are cooking, prepare the zucchini noodles by spiralizing or cutting them into thin strips.
7. Heat olive oil in a pan over medium-high heat and add minced garlic.
8. Cook for about 1 minute, until fragrant.
9. Add the zucchini noodles to the pan and sauté for 3-5 minutes, until slightly softened.
10. In a separate pan, heat olive oil over medium heat and add diced tomatoes and minced garlic. Simmer for 5-7 minutes until the sauce thickens.
11. Once the meatballs are done baking, add them to the marinara sauce and cook for an additional 2-3 minutes until coated in sauce.
12. Serve the turkey meatballs on top of the zucchini noodles with extra marinara sauce on top if desired.

Grilled Chicken Caesar Salad with a Light Vinaigrette

Ingredients:

- 1 lb boneless, skinless chicken breasts
- Salt and pepper
- Olive oil
- Romaine lettuce, chopped
- Croutons (optional)

For the dressing:

- 3 tbsp olive oil
- 2 cloves of garlic, minced
- 1 tsp Dijon mustard
- Juice of half a lemon
- Salt and pepper to taste

Instructions:

1. Start by seasoning the chicken breasts with salt and pepper on both sides.
2. Heat a grill or grill pan over medium-high heat and brush with olive oil.
3. Grill the chicken for about 6-7 minutes per side, or until fully cooked (reaching an internal temperature of 165 degrees F).

4. While the chicken is cooking, prepare the dressing by combining olive oil, minced garlic, Dijon mustard, lemon juice, salt, and pepper in a small bowl.
5. Whisk together until well combined.
6. Once the chicken is done cooking, let it rest for a few minutes before slicing into strips.
7. In a large bowl, mix together the chopped romaine lettuce and dressing until well coated.
8. Serve the grilled chicken on top of the dressed romaine lettuce, and add croutons if desired. Enjoy!

Sweet Potato and Black Bean Tacos

Ingredients:

- 2 large sweet potatoes, peeled and chopped into small cubes
- Olive oil
- Salt and pepper
- 1 can black beans, drained and rinsed
- 1 tsp chili powder
- 1 tsp cumin
- ½ tsp garlic powder
- Corn tortillas

Optional toppings:

- Avocado slices
- Shredded cheese (vegan or dairy)
- Salsa

Instructions:

1. Preheat the oven to 375 degrees F.
2. Line a baking sheet with parchment paper.
3. Place the cubed sweet potatoes on the baking sheet and drizzle with olive oil, salt, and pepper.
4. Toss until evenly coated.
5. Bake for 25-30 minutes, or until the sweet potatoes are tender and lightly browned.

6. While the sweet potatoes are cooking, prepare the black beans by heating them in a small saucepan over medium heat with chili powder, cumin, and garlic powder. Stir occasionally until heated through.
7. Warm up corn tortillas on a skillet or in the oven according to package instructions.
8. Assemble your tacos by filling each tortilla with roasted sweet potatoes, black beans, and any desired toppings such as avocado slices, shredded cheese, and salsa.
9. Serve hot and enjoy!

The recipes provided for the Rosacea diet not only showcase a variety of flavourful and nutritious options but also prioritize ingredients that are gentle on the skin while promoting overall health.

Conclusion

As you reach the end of this guide on managing rosacea through diet and lifestyle changes, it's important to take a moment to reflect on the journey you're embarking on. By choosing to educate yourself and make conscious decisions about your health, you are taking significant steps towards improving your quality of life and managing your rosacea more effectively. Your dedication and commitment are commendable, and it's clear you are ready to make positive changes that can lead to long-lasting results.

Managing rosacea is not just about avoiding certain foods or adopting specific skincare routines; it's about embracing a holistic approach that encompasses your entire lifestyle. The choices you make daily, from the foods you eat to the way you handle stress, all play a crucial role in how well you manage this condition. By focusing on anti-inflammatory foods, you can reduce flare-ups and soothe your skin. Incorporating nutrient-rich vegetables, lean proteins, and healthy fats into your diet can provide your body with the essential vitamins and minerals it needs to maintain healthy skin.

Beyond diet, lifestyle changes are equally important. Stress management, for instance, is a vital component of rosacea management. High levels of stress can trigger flare-ups, so finding effective ways to relax and unwind is crucial. Whether it's through yoga, meditation, spending time in nature, or simply engaging in hobbies you love, reducing stress can have a profound impact on your skin's health.

Hydration is another key factor in managing rosacea. Drinking plenty of water helps keep your skin hydrated and can prevent dryness and irritation. Additionally, paying attention to the products you use on your skin can make a significant difference. Opt for gentle, fragrance-free cleansers and moisturizers that are specifically designed for sensitive skin. Avoiding harsh chemicals and abrasive exfoliants can help maintain your skin's barrier and reduce the risk of irritation.

One of the most important aspects of managing rosacea is listening to your body. Keep track of foods, activities, and environmental factors that seem to trigger your symptoms. By identifying and understanding your triggers, you can make informed decisions that help minimize flare-ups. This personalized approach allows you to tailor your diet and lifestyle to what works best for you.

It's also beneficial to seek support and connect with others who understand what you're going through. Joining a support group or online community can provide you with valuable insights, tips, and encouragement. Sharing your experiences and learning from others can be incredibly empowering and can help you feel less isolated in your journey.

Remember, managing rosacea is a marathon, not a sprint. It requires patience, persistence, and a positive mindset. There will be days when you face challenges, but each step you take towards a healthier lifestyle brings you closer to more manageable symptoms and greater overall well-being. Celebrate your progress, no matter how small, and continue to prioritize self-care.

Thank you for taking the time to read through this guide. Your willingness to learn and make changes is a testament to your resilience and determination. By implementing these diet and lifestyle strategies, you are empowering yourself to take control of your rosacea and improve your quality of life.

FAQs

What foods should I avoid to prevent rosacea flare-ups?

To minimize rosacea flare-ups, avoid spicy foods, hot beverages, alcohol (especially red wine), and foods high in histamines such as aged cheeses, processed meats, and fermented products. These items can dilate blood vessels and trigger redness and inflammation.

Are there any specific foods that can help reduce rosacea symptoms?

Yes, anti-inflammatory foods can help manage rosacea symptoms. Incorporate fruits like blueberries, vegetables such as spinach and kale, lean proteins like fish and chicken, and healthy fats from sources such as avocados and olive oil. These foods can help soothe your skin and reduce inflammation.

Can drinking plenty of water help with rosacea?

Absolutely. Staying well-hydrated is essential for maintaining skin health. Drinking plenty of water helps keep your skin hydrated, reducing dryness and irritation, which are common issues for people with rosacea.

How can I identify which foods are my personal triggers?

Keep a food diary to track what you eat and note any rosacea flare-ups. Over time, you may notice patterns that help you identify specific triggers. This personalized approach allows you to adjust your diet according to what works best for you.

Is it safe to drink coffee if I have rosacea?

Hot beverages, including coffee, can trigger rosacea for some people. If you notice flare-ups after drinking coffee, try switching to iced coffee or herbal teas. Monitor your symptoms to determine if caffeine or the temperature of the beverage is the primary trigger.

Can supplements help manage rosacea symptoms?

Certain supplements like omega-3 fatty acids, vitamin D, and probiotics may help reduce inflammation and support skin health. However, it's crucial to consult with a healthcare provider before adding any supplements to your regimen to ensure they are safe and appropriate for you.

How important is stress management in controlling rosacea?

Stress is a significant trigger for many people with rosacea. Incorporating stress-reducing activities such as yoga, meditation, deep-breathing exercises, or spending time in nature can help manage your symptoms. Finding effective ways to relax and unwind is crucial for keeping flare-ups in check.

References and Helpful Links

News-Medical. (2019, February 27). Rosacea and small intestinal bacterial overgrowth (SIBO).
https://www.news-medical.net/health/Rosacea-and-Small-Intestinal-Bacterial-Overgrowth.aspx#:~:text=Rosacea%20and%20Gut%20Symptoms,out%20of%20every%2010%20patients.

Rosacea - Symptoms and causes - Mayo Clinic. (2023, October 17). Mayo Clinic.
https://www.mayoclinic.org/diseases-conditions/rosacea/symptoms-causes/syc-20353815

Branch, N. S. C. a. O. (2024, July 19). Rosacea. National Institute of Arthritis and Musculoskeletal and Skin Diseases.
https://www.niams.nih.gov/health-topics/rosacea#:~:text=Scientists%20do%20not%20know%20what,fully%20understand%20why%20inflammation%20occurs.

Types of rosacea. (n.d.). NYU Langone Health.
https://nyulangone.org/conditions/rosacea/types#:~:text=Papulopustular%20Rosacea&text=These%20typically%20appear%20on%20the,long%20time%20to%20go%20away.

Rosacea - Diagnosis and treatment - Mayo Clinic. (2023, October 17).
https://www.mayoclinic.org/diseases-conditions/rosacea/diagnosis-treatment/drc-20353820

News-Medical. (2023b, July 21). Lifestyle changes for rosacea. https://www.news-medical.net/health/Lifestyle-Changes-for-Rosacea.aspx

DermaHarmony. (2019, March 21). Rosacea Diet (1800 calories) - DermaHarmony. https://www.dermaharmony.com/pages/rosacea-meal-plan-1800

Rd, J. B. M. (2023, August 9). The best and worst foods for rosacea. EatingWell. https://www.eatingwell.com/article/7906387/best-worst-foods-for-rosacea/

www.ingramcontent.com/pod-product-compliance
Lightning Source LLC
LaVergne TN
LVHW012032060526
838201LV00061B/4565